The Carnival

story by Kaye Umansky
illustrated by Steve Smallman

It wasn't a good day.
Mouse and Jojo had to look after Pip.
Pip was in a bad mood.
He cried and cried.

Then he cried some more.

"Shall we take him to the park?"
said Sam as they got in the lift.
"Do you want to go to the park, Pip?"
asked Jojo.
"Noooooo!" wailed Pip.
He waved his arms around.

One small hand hit the magic button!

WHOOOSH!

"Oh no!" said Mouse. "We can't take
Pip to Strange Street. He's too little.
Quick, let's go back down!"
But Pip had his own ideas.
He heard music. He saw balloons.
He wanted to stay.
"Noooooo!" he yelled.
"Just for a little while then," said Jojo.
"But you must be good."

Strange Street was having a carnival!
The children ran to get a good view.
There was a band marching down
the street. There were clowns and
a man on stilts.

A clown gave Pip a red balloon.
That made him happy.

There was a long line of floats,
pulled by horses.
"Look!" shouted Sam, pointing at the
first one. "There's the dragon that scared
me the first time I came."
"And there's the man that gave me the
strange sweets," said Mouse.

The man from the sweet shop waved merrily.
Pip waved back.
The dragon breathed fire.
"Again!" said Pip. "Again!"

The next float was full of people in space suits.
"There's the buggy man!" shouted Mouse.
"Remember our adventure on the moon?"
"How could we forget it?" said Ben.
They all waved to the buggy man.
He gave them a wink.

Jojo liked the next float.
It was full of cowboys.
The little boy she had saved
was there with his mother.
"Hello Jojo!" he shouted.
"Thanks for saving me!"

Along came a float with knights in armour, and ladies wearing long dresses and tall hats. The red knight and the green knight waved to Ben.
"How are you feeling, Ben?" they called.
"Is your head better?"
"Fine!" called Ben.
Pip jumped up and down.
He was so excited.

"Oh no!" said Sam.
"Look what's coming next!"
Nobody liked the next float much.
It was a big sailing ship,
full of ugly pirates.
Jake and the Captain were there.
The Captain was looking through
a telescope.

When he saw the children, he shook his fist.
The children tried to look small.
"Bad man!" shouted Pip.
"Shush Pip!" said the children.
But Pip just giggled.

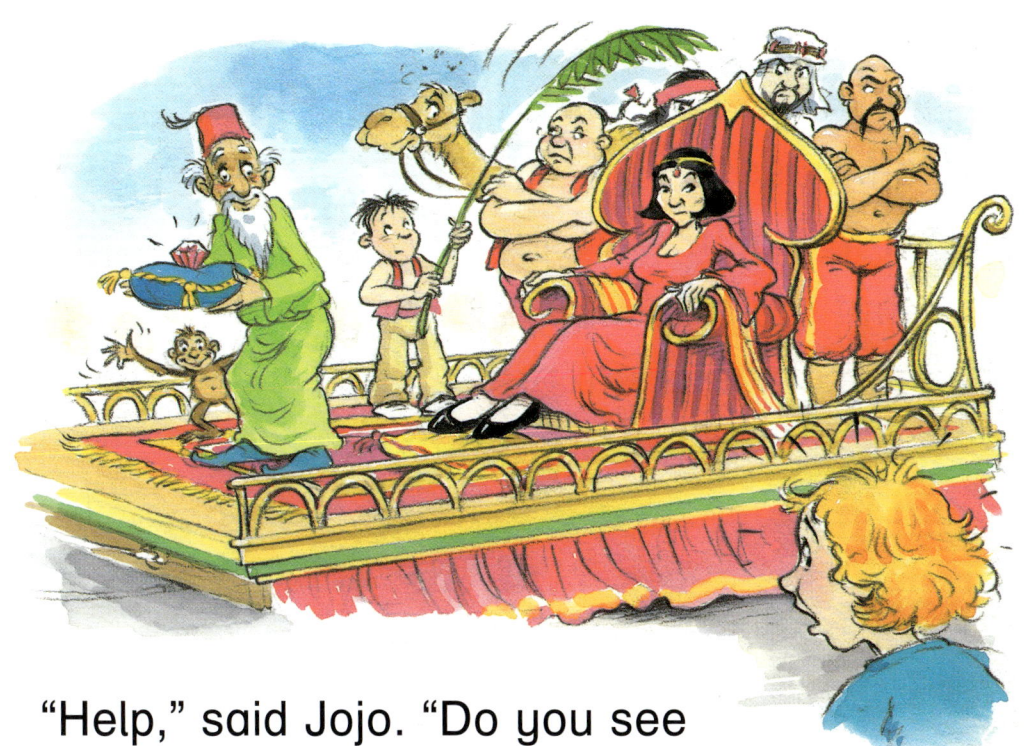

"Help," said Jojo. "Do you see who I see?"
The next float carried the Red Queen with her band of thieves.
The old man was there too, holding the Rose Red Ruby.
"Thank you for helping, children!" he called as he went by.
The Red Queen glared at them.

"Bad lady!" shouted Pip. "Go away!"
"I do wish you would be quiet, Pip,"
said Mouse.
But Pip was having fun.
"Is that the end?" asked Jojo.
"Here comes one more," said Ben,
"but it seems to be empty."

The empty float
stopped next to them.
"This is for you," said the driver.
"Hop on."

The children climbed on the float.
The crowds cheered as they made
their way up the street.
Pip was laughing and clapping
his hands.

"We had better take him home when we reach the lift," said Jojo.
"He gets sick when he's too excited."

They got off at the lift.
"Goodbye," shouted everyone.
"Come back to Strange Street one day!"
"We will," promised the children.

"Well, that cheered you up, didn't it Pip?"
said Sam, when they landed.
But Pip's lovely red balloon had gone.
He opened his mouth and said ...

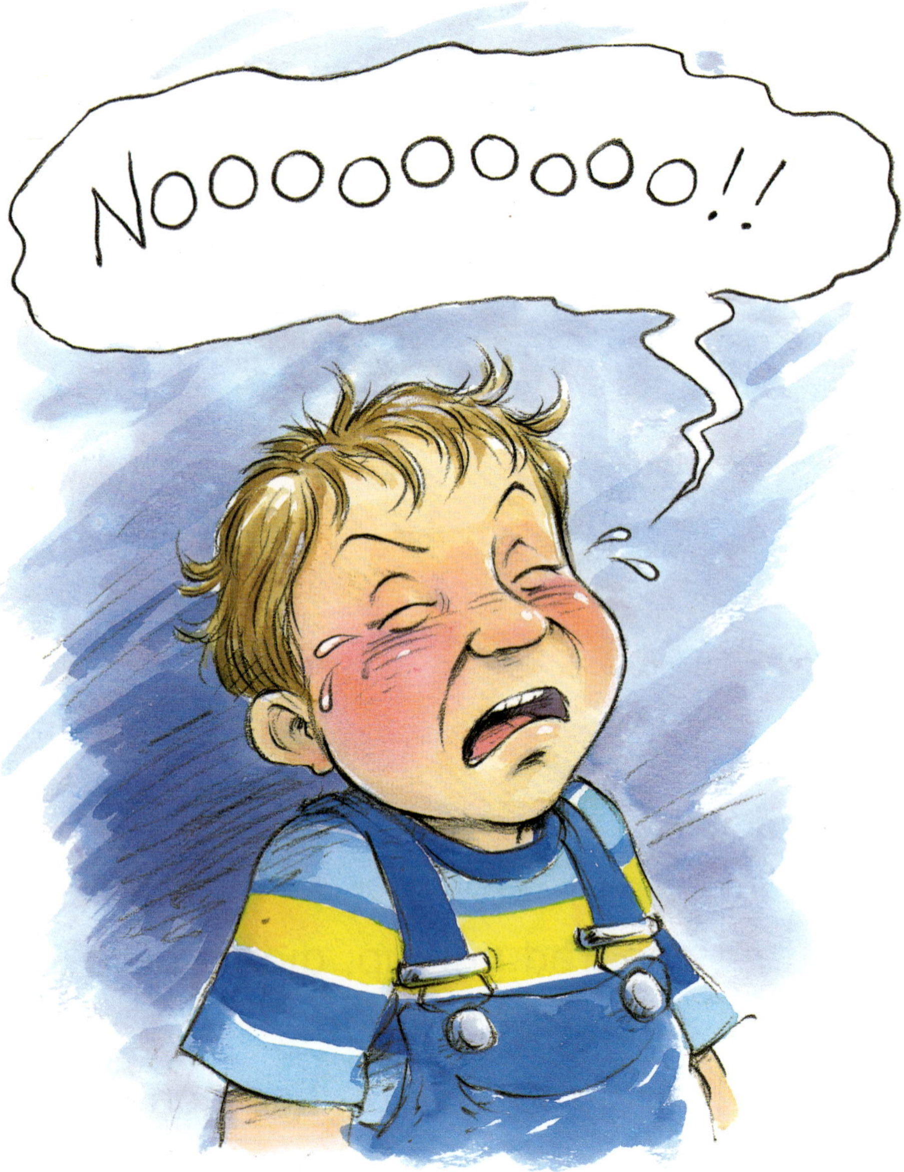
NOOOOOOOOO!!